21st-CENTURY ECONOMICS

UNDERSTANDING INFLATION

CHET'LA SEBREE

Cavendish
Square
New York

Published in 2020 by Cavendish Square Publishing, LLC
243 5th Avenue, Suite 136, New York, NY 10016

Library of Congress Cataloging-in-Publication Data

Names: Sebree, Chet'la, author.
Title: Understanding inflation / Chet'la Sebree.
Description: First edition. | New York : Cavendish Square, 2020. |
Series: 21st-century economics | Includes bibliographical references and index.
Identifiers: LCCN 2018051969 (print) | LCCN 2018055699 (ebook) |
ISBN 9781502646019 (ebook) | ISBN 9781502646002 (library bound) |
ISBN 9781502645999 (pbk.)
Subjects: LCSH: Inflation (Finance)--Juvenile literature. |
Economics--Juvenile literature.
Classification: LCC HG229 (ebook) | LCC HG229 .S376 2020 (print) |
DDC 332.4/1--dc23
LC record available at https://lccn.loc.gov/2018051969

Editorial Director: David McNamara
Copy Editor: Nathan Heidelberger
Associate Art Director: Alan Sliwinski
Designer: Joe Parenteau
Production Coordinator: Karol Szymczuk
Photo Research: J8 Media

Portions of this book originally appeared in *How Inflation Works* by Joyce Hart.

Printed in the United States of America

CONTENTS

ECONOMIC INFLATION

In economic terms, inflation refers to a steady increase in the price of goods (like food and gasoline) and services (like hospitals and public transportation). For instance, when there is inflation, the cost of food is higher than it was the year before. Similarly, it requires more money to fill the gas tank of the family car. And although you have been saving your money for that pair of jeans you saw at the store last winter, this winter those jeans might be out of your price range if there is high inflation.

Opposite: Too much air in a balloon can threaten its structure and cause it to burst. In the same way, the rise in prices over time, known as inflation, can be dangerous for economies.

Positive and Negative Effects of Inflation

While inflation may sound like a bad thing for the economy, under some conditions inflation is good. Inflation can help boost businesses' profits, or the money that businesses make after paying all of their bills. If a company can charge a little more for its goods, it will be able to make more money. This boost, in turn, helps the economy. If a business makes extra money, the owners might share those profits with their employees.

For instance, your parents might come home and say they got raises. This means they are now making more money. To celebrate, your parents might buy a new car or computer. When your parents and other people purchase new items, the stores from which they bought those goods also celebrate. They are making more money too.

Many economists believe a healthy rate of inflation is around a 3 percent increase each year. The rate of inflation is the average increase in the cost of goods and services over a set period of time. So, a 3 percent rate of inflation each year means that prices rise from one year to the next at a rate of 3 percent, or three pennies per dollar spent. So, if it costs you $10 to buy a book this year, next year that same book will cost $10.30. A 3 percent rise in inflation is not difficult to handle for most people who have a job.

It is normal for prices to rise over time; however, it is problematic if these prices rise too quickly.

If inflation is not controlled, however, the economy can suffer. If prices on goods continue to rise and your parents' salaries do not increase, then new cars, new computers, and even food can cost more money than they can afford. To give you an example of how this might work in your own life, let's imagine a situation.

Amani's Lemonade Stand

Suppose you have a friend named Amani whose family owns a lemon orchard. Last summer, she set up a lemonade stand and sold some of the best lemonade you'd ever tasted. You and all your neighbors bought glasses of lemonade faster than Amani could make it. This year, Amani decides to raise the price from $1 to $2 per glass. The first time you go to the stand, you are shocked by this inflated price. However, you are very thirsty, so you pay the extra dollar.

But as the summer goes along, you and your neighbors start complaining about the high price. Everyone feels the lemonade is too expensive, so you all stop going to the stand. Amani sits there all day, waiting for people to

Goods and services account for most things you spend money on, from lemonade and jeans to home repairs and travel.

come. All the lemonade goes bad, and she has to throw it away. This goes on for a week. Eventually, Amani figures it out. She finally realizes that she has to lower her price to bring her customers back to the stand. Amani puts up new signs advertising that the price has been cut in half. You and your neighbors start buying lemonade again. Soon, Amani's business is once again thriving.

The Bigger Picture

Economies of large countries like the United States are not quite as simple as Amani's lemonade stand. However, some of the same economic principles apply. Businesses will raise their prices in hopes of making a bigger profit; however, people can't always afford these new, inflated prices. Businesses have to then lower their prices in hopes of bringing back their customers. Sometimes this works. Other times it doesn't, which can have dangerous effects on businesses and economies.

The federal government is responsible for making sure these upward and downward shifts don't get out of control, as both very high and very low inflation rates aren't good for the economy. It constantly monitors the prices of goods and services in hopes of keeping them affordable because an economy can only do well when people can afford to buy not only the things they need but the things they want.

CHAPTER 1

THE CAUSES OF INFLATION

Inflation is more than just an increase in the cost of goods and services. For economists to declare that a country's economy is in a state of inflation, the price of these goods and services needs to both rise significantly and remain at this higher price for an extended period of time. So, for instance, the short-lived rise in prices at Amani's lemonade stand would not be a sign of an inflated economy. It was a profit-driven increase.

Profit-Driven Increase

A profit-driven increase happens when a business's expenses haven't changed but the company increases its prices anyway. For instance, the price of a movie ticket might increase from $6 to $9 over a period of two years.

Opposite: High inflation can lead to the costs of goods and services outweighing the value of your money.

However, this does not necessarily mean that the economy is suffering the effects of inflation. It might just mean that the owner of the movie theater wants to make a bigger profit. The theater owner might hope that people want to see movies badly enough that they will pay the extra money for tickets.

The price he or she charges rises even though operating expenses have not risen at the same rate. Operating expenses for a movie theater would include things like the price of utilities like electricity and concessions like popcorn and soda. If the operating costs stay the same, then the ticket price increase has nothing to do with helping the business stay open. Instead of being a necessity, the price increase is a profit-driven choice.

However, if the owner raises prices because the cost of operating the business has increased, the price increase could be a sign of inflation, particularly if ticket prices remain high for a long period of time.

Cost-Push Inflation

Cost-push inflation occurs when a company's expenses increase. These increases might be for a variety of reasons. A company may have to pay higher taxes to the government or higher wages to its employees. Similarly, the cost of supplies that the company uses to make its goods or provide its services might have increased.

Cost-push inflation occurs when a company has to raise its prices because its cost of doing business has increased.

For example, let's say that Amani had three major new costs before she could open her lemonade stand this year. First, the wood in her old stand rotted, so she had to build a new one. The wood was expensive, costing her $30. Second, last year she received a notice from the city stating that she would have to buy a permit. The permit, which gives Amani the city's permission to sell lemonade on the street, cost $15. Third, last summer some people complained that the lemonade was too warm. So, Amani bought a cooler to keep ice for her customers. This cost her another $15. Her total added costs were $60.

In order to make as much money as she did last year, Amani calculates that she has to raise the cost of each glass of lemonade to $1.50. The extra costs that Amani had to pay for the new supplies and the permit have pushed up, or inflated, the price of her lemonade. Without raising the price, Amani will run the risk of the costs for business eating into her profits.

Another good example of this is the airline business. In 2008, when the price of gasoline doubled, the airline business had to pay a lot more money to buy supplies (expensive gasoline to fuel the planes). In order to pay for fuel, the airlines raised the cost of airline tickets. They also added extra charges for services that used to be free, like a cost for checking in suitcases. These extra charges helped the airlines cover their costs. The higher prices for the airline tickets were the result of cost-push inflation.

Demand-Pull Inflation

Demand-pull inflation occurs when a lot of people want to buy something but there are not enough goods or services available. Let's go back to Amani's lemonade stand to understand how an increase in demand can result in higher prices.

According to the law of supply and demand, as demand increases, so do prices.

It was a hard winter for Amani's parents' orchard. A late-winter frost killed many of the lemons. So when Amani's neighbors come to the lemonade stand in the summer, they find only one pitcher of lemonade per day. The first day, Amani sells ten glasses of lemonade, but there were fifteen people who stood in line. This means that five people go home without quenching their thirst.

Those five people who did not get the lemonade the first day rush to Amani's stand very early the next morning. They want to make sure they are first in line. But the news has gotten out that there is only a small supply of lemonade this year. For this reason, another twenty people come running to Amani's stand. They hope to get a taste of the lemonade before the supply runs out. Again, Amani has only enough lemonade for ten people. So, fifteen people go home empty-handed.

On the third day, even more people show up at the stand. There is some pushing and shoving going on for the first ten places in line. Amani realizes that her lemonade is in high demand. She changes her price from $1 to $2 per glass. Some people leave because they refuse to pay the 100 percent inflated price. However, ten people stay and pay the doubled price. Amani makes a big profit.

In this example, the demand for the lemonade pulls the price up, causing the inflation. This type of inflation often happens in business, especially when a new product first comes out on the market. This happened when Nintendo released its long awaited new gaming system: Wii. So many people wanted to buy the Wii that Nintendo could not keep up with the demand. So, the price of the Wii remained high. Once most of the orders for the Wii were met and not as many people wanted to buy it, then the company could lower the price to encourage less excited customers to buy it.

Purchasing Power

Economists identify inflation in different ways. One of the ways is to calculate how much purchasing or buying power consumers are enjoying. For example, economists might measure if $50 buys as much food today as it did two years ago. If their research reveals that it does, then there has been no inflation in the food market.

However, they might not end their research there. They might ask other questions, like if $50 purchases as much gasoline as it did two years ago. Similarly, they might examine the price of clothing or how much it costs to visit a doctor. If they find significant price increases in any of the major categories of goods or services, then they analyze the results further.

They will want to know how big the price increases are and how these increases are affecting families. Even if food prices are not inflated, the inflated costs of other

THE REGULATION OF INFLATION

In the United States, the Federal Reserve is responsible for monitoring and regulating inflation. It is the central bank of the United States. Under the direction of Congress, the Federal Reserve sets the rules for US banks in addition to setting interest rates. An interest rate is the rate at which a bank makes a profit from someone who borrows money. These rates affect inflation.

When interest rates are low, people are encouraged to borrow money to buy things that they want. For instance, if you wanted to buy a computer game that cost $50 and all you had was $20, you might make a deal with a friend to borrow the extra $30 that you need. You might tell your friend that instead of just paying her back the $30, you will pay back $31.50. In this way, your friend can make $1.50 without doing anything except lending you the money. This chance to make some extra money might convince her to agree to the deal. You are paying her back at a 5 percent interest rate. The extra $1.50 that you have to pay her—5 percent of the amount you want to borrow—will not be that difficult for you. So, you go buy the computer game. In a month, you pay back the $31.50.

When bank interest rates are low, people are more likely to buy big-ticket items like houses or cars. However, if a lot of people are looking for houses to buy and not that many houses are for sale, then the price of houses rises, or becomes inflated.

Although the Federal Reserve is headquartered in Washington, DC, there are twelve reserve banks located in cities throughout the United States.

When the Federal Reserve sees that inflation is rising, it raises interest rates. Where interest rates for borrowing money might have been at 5 percent a year, the Federal Reserve might raise the rate to 7 percent. Whereas a lot of people might have been able to afford a loan at 5 percent interest, when the interest rates reach 7 percent or more, fewer people can afford to take out a loan. This is because it will be more expensive to pay back that loan. A $100,000 loan with a 5 percent annual interest rate would cost $125,000 to pay back in five years. A 7 percent interest rate would boost that total to $135,000. When interest rates rise, the demand for loans, as well as the demand for new houses, begins to decrease. When the demand decreases, prices fall, as does inflation. This is one of the ways in which the Federal Reserve regulates inflation.

The exchange of money for goods and services is the foundation of any economy.

goods and services might be causing families serious financial difficulties.

Devalued Currency

Inflation is also affected by the amount of paper currency in circulation. This is the total amount of money that is being exchanged and used in a country. The more money that a government prints and has in circulation, the less value that money has. The less value that money has, the higher prices rise because greater amounts of the less valuable currency are needed to buy things. This concept is called devaluation.

As a practical example of how devalued currency works, imagine that you own one of the rarest cards in the whole Pokémon series. What would you be willing to trade for this rare card? Now, imagine that everyone just learned that this rare card you own has been duplicated by the company that makes Pokémon cards. Instead of there being just one hundred cards in the world, there are now one hundred million of them. Because the company made so many copies of this once-rare card, the value of your Pokémon card has just been devalued. People would be far less willing to exchange a lot of cards for your card that can now be purchased easily.

This same idea works with a nation's currency. Paper money is valued because of standards that a country sets for those paper bills. For instance, let's look at the dollar. Imagine the United States prints ten thousand dollar bills made of paper. The paper is not worth anything by itself. However, if the US government guarantees that one dollar stands for one ounce of silver and promises that it has ten thousand ounces of silver available in its bank, then a paper bill is worth something. One dollar is worth one ounce of silver.

But one year later, let's say that the government wants to increase its currency, so it prints ten thousand more dollars. Unfortunately, the US government does not have ten thousand more ounces of silver to back up this

Different precious metals, such as gold and silver, have been used to back the value of paper currency.

new printing of dollar bills. This means that each of the combined twenty thousand bills is now worth only one-half an ounce of silver. Although a citizen of this country might have been able to buy a bike for fifty dollars last year, that same bike now costs one hundred dollars. Imagine how much less a dollar would be worth if the government had printed one million more dollars without increasing the amount of silver in its bank to back up the currency. Unfortunately, this dangerous situation happens.

CHAPTER 2

UNDERSTANDING CURRENCY AND INFLATION

Inflation predates paper currency as we know it. People used to barter, or trade, goods and services for other goods and services. For example, a goat herder might barter with a farmer by offering goats' milk or goats' cheese in exchange for the farmer's corn or wheat. A tailor might offer to make a new suit of clothes for a livestock owner in exchange for a horse. As time went by and the populations of towns began to grow, pulling a horse all over town or chasing a herd of sheep through the city streets to barter with became more difficult and inconvenient. So, bartering was not always the best, most efficient way to purchase goods or services. This is when money came into use. But money did not always take the

Opposite: Currencies from around the world have different values based on the strength of each country's economy.

form of coins and paper bills as it does today. In fact, one kind of early money took the form of seashells.

Early Currency

In many ancient cultures, shells were prized possessions. They were used just as people use money today. The shells were different from one culture to another, but they all worked in the same way. Everything that a person might need could be exchanged for a certain number of shells.

Before the creation of modern-day coins and banknotes, ancient peoples used shells, like the cowrie shells pictured here, as currency.

It wasn't until later, sometime around 4000 BCE, that gold was first used as money. At first, gold nuggets were used. The nuggets had to be weighed during each transaction to guarantee their worth. The more the nugget weighed, the more it was worth. Over time, instead of using gold nuggets of random weights, the gold was melted into the form of bars that had a uniform weight. This meant that the gold didn't have to be weighed during each exchange. Although using gold bars was more convenient that pulling a wagon of chickens into town, they were still heavy.

Later, silver was introduced as a prized currency. Sometimes gold and silver were made in the form of rings that could be worn on a person's fingers or carried on leather strings. People used the gold and silver rings like we use coins and paper money today.

It wasn't until around the seventh century BCE, that gold and silver were made into coins. But the coins were not all made of gold and silver. Other metals, such as bronze, copper, and tin, were also used by ancient cultures. For a while, China even used leather coins.

Coins were also used by the Greeks and the Romans, who mixed cheaper metals in with their gold and silver coins when they needed more money. The less gold and silver in the coins, the less value the coins had. Mixing in cheaper metals in order to be able to make more coins is the same as today's practice of printing more money without having any additional value to back the new bills. Just like in modern economies, the Greeks and the Romans suffered from inflation when they devalued the coins in this way. As the coins lost value, more coins were needed to purchase goods and services. That was when inflation set in.

Paper Currency

The Chinese were the first to issue paper money during the Tang dynasty between 618 and 907 CE. They created paper bills because they were running low on copper, the main metal they used for their coins. Their paper bills were based on real worth. They were backed by reserves, or supplies, of precious metals. As in other countries, however, when the Chinese people needed more money, they just printed more paper bills. They no longer backed the bills with the same amount of real wealth. The paper money began to lose its worth. As in so many instances in which countries increased their money supply without maintaining its worth, inflation in China soared. In 1455, the country eliminated paper currency to halt inflation. China wouldn't adopt it again for a few hundred years.

This sort of quick rise in inflation has happened throughout history. For instance, the American colonies

The continental was the paper currency used by Americans during the Revolutionary War. This 1778 note was backed by gold and silver.

produced paper money called continentals during the American Revolution (1775–1783). The production of this paper currency was managed by the Continental Congress, the governing body of the original thirteen colonies before and during the war. At first, the Congress promised that the continentals would be backed by silver. However, as the war dragged on, the army's expenses grew. In response, the Congress printed continentals far beyond the amount of silver they had to back them. By the end of the war, the paper money was almost worthless.

WARTIME INFLATION

One of the first serious occurrences of inflation in the United States was the result of the American Revolution. However, the changing value of money and wartime inflation are common occurrences. For instance, some currency can become completely useless after a war. This is what happened to Confederate currency after the Civil War. At the war's end, the Confederacy no longer existed. This meant that Confederate money had no worth at all.

Inflation can have many different wartime causes. It's not always caused by the government printing more

When a country collapses, its money becomes worthless. This means that some people lose all of their wealth. This is what happened to those with banknotes from the Confederate States of America after the Civil War.

money. For instance, sometimes a government borrows money from another country for war supplies. When the war is over, that government has to pay back the money it borrowed plus interest. Remember, if you borrowed $10 from a bank, the bank might charge you 10 percent interest. This means that you would have to pay back the $10 you borrowed plus the interest, which would be an additional $1.

Now, imagine if a country borrowed $1 million. Ten percent interest would be $100,000. By the end of a war, a government might owe so much money that it has trouble paying it back. The government might then decide to raise taxes on things like gasoline to collect more money to pay back the loan. Higher taxes often mean a price increase for goods and services. If there are higher taxes on things like gas, companies often have to pay more to make and ship their products. This causes cost-push inflation. As the companies' expenses rises, so do the prices of their goods and services so that the company can still make a profit.

The Introduction of the Gold Standard

Although paper money was used in Europe and in the North American colonies in earlier centuries, it wasn't until 1821 that a gold standard was set for the paper bills. The government in England was the first to set gold

The gold standard meant that each banknote could be redeemed for a specific amount of gold. However, many countries abandoned the gold standard in light of the financial devastation caused by World War I and the Great Depression.

as the standard value backing paper money. It did this to stop the inflation that had arisen due to banks printing paper money and randomly setting its value, rather than basing the value on actual gold or silver. Most early paper money was more like a promise from the bank that the bills could be exchanged for a certain amount of precious metal. But the banks offered no guarantee that this would actually happen before the gold standard was made the rule.

With the gold standard established in England, each paper bill had a specific value in gold. In 1900, the United States passed the Gold Standard Act. It meant that paper money in America could officially be redeemed for gold. This standard was, however, abandoned by many countries after World War I and the Great Depression left countries in financial ruins in the early twentieth century.

Strength of a Country's Currency

Today, the gold standard no longer exists in either Europe or the United States. Instead, the US dollar is based on the potential wealth of the country and the performance of the US economy relative to other countries. American citizens and businesses must pay taxes, for instance, and those taxes become the basis for some of the country's potential wealth. So, as long as the US economy is doing well, the US dollar is considered strong.

But when the economy is not doing well—when the country's potential to generate wealth decreases—the US dollar loses its strength. In general, the dollar is worth less during economic downturns than it is when the economy is doing well. Because all currencies around the world are not based on the same gold standard, or are not based on any gold standard at all, the worth of a country's currency constantly rises and falls, depending on how well the country's economy is doing.

For most of the twenty-first century, the pound sterling, the official currency in the United Kingdom, was stronger than the US dollar. For instance, in 2008, the US dollar's strength was so low that it took almost two US dollars to equal one pound in the United Kingdom. This was in part due to the Great Recession, a period of economic downturn between 2008 and 2009. This recession affected people globally because many economies are linked by trade. Despite the global effect of the recession, the US dollar suffered in comparison to the pound and the euro, the currency in most of Europe.

The strength of a country's currency can constantly shift, however. These shifts can occur for many reasons including a country's political decisions. For instance, in June 2016, the United Kingdom voted to leave the European Union (EU). The EU is an economic and political organization made up of several countries in Europe.

The UK leaving the EU would be like California leaving the United States. The decision had major effects on the country's economy and the strength of its currency. In the aftermath of the decision, the UK's central bank pumped money into the economy and lowered interest rates. Although this kept the country afloat following the decision, it devalued the currency. By October 2016, the pound equaled only 1.18 US dollars. It was the lowest the pound's strength had fallen in over thirty years.

Although the worth of currency is not simply backed in precious metals anymore, the control over its printing and circulation remains important. It is just one of the key elements to regulating inflation. Equally as important are each country's political decisions and the global markets.

CHAPTER 3

HOW IT'S MEASURED

Despite the importance of tracking inflation rates, they are actually quite difficult to measure. In the United States, this difficulty comes from the fact that the cost of living is different across the country. For instance, in February 2016, gas was $2.63 per gallon in Hawaii, whereas it was $1.39 per gallon in Oklahoma. Additionally, to measure inflation, the US government only looks at the cost of living in cities, even though the cost of living is generally higher in cities than in more suburban or rural areas. For these reasons, it takes concentrated effort for the government to determine what constitutes inflation.

Opposite: The Department of Labor in Washington, DC, plays a major role in helping the US government understand economic trends.

The Consumer Price Index

The Department of Labor is responsible for collecting and analyzing a lot of the information that helps the US federal government determine what is happening with the economy. Through the information the agency collects, it is able to produce what is called the consumer price index (CPI). The CPI is used to gauge the average change over time of how much people are spending on goods and services. The department does this by selecting specific goods and services that are routinely purchased by consumers.

The Market Basket

The Department of Labor collects information about the buying patterns of people who live in cities. They send surveys to urban consumers and urban wage earners. This group, according to the Department of Labor, represents about 93 percent of the entire population of the United States. The department also sends surveys to people who are unemployed, people who run their own businesses, and people who are retired. People who live in rural areas of the country, such as farming families, and people who are in the military are not included in the surveys. From this information, the Department of Labor creates a market basket. This is not a real basket. It is a representation of the most popular items people in the United States pay for each year.

The market basket, though not a real basket, is made up of popular items on which people spend money, including groceries.

To create the market basket, the Department of Labor asks several thousand people to participate. For instance, in 2013 and 2014, about twenty-four thousand consumers provided information about their spending habits each year. Additionally, another twelve thousand consumers each year were asked to keep daily logs of what they purchased during a two-week period. The Department of Labor then takes these reports and studies the goods and services that are listed. The department gives certain items that appear frequently more importance than others that appear infrequently. The next step is to choose the most important items. It is these most frequently purchased goods and services that are put into the market basket.

The market basket items fall into several distinct categories. These categories are:

- Food and beverages—This includes goods such as milk, coffee, chicken, and snacks.
- Housing—This includes the money people pay for rent, utilities, and furniture.
- Clothing—This includes clothing as well as jewelry.
- Transportation—This includes new and used cars, fares for airlines, public transportation, gasoline, and car insurance.
- Medical care—This includes doctor visits, medications, eyeglasses, and other medical services.
- Recreation—This includes television, sports equipment, pets and pet supplies, and movie tickets.
- Education and communication—This includes college tuition, telephone services, and computer software.
- Other goods and services—This includes everything from haircuts and other personal services to funeral expenses.

There are additional items that the Department of Labor includes, such as taxes people pay when they buy certain goods and services and money spent on things

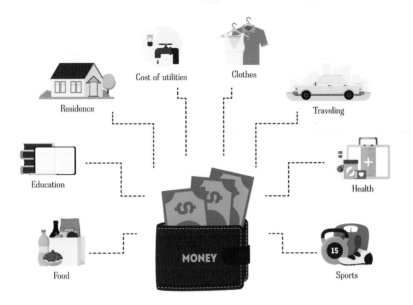

A variety of goods and services people pay for, such as health care, utilities, and entertainment, are included in the fixed list that becomes the market basket.

like water and sewage bills. Items that are not included are taxes on people's wages (income tax) or money that people spend on investments (like stocks and bonds), real estate (land and houses or apartments), or life insurance.

How Does the Market Basket Measure Inflation?

Once the market basket is set, the Department of Labor employs people who either visit or call thousands of stores, manufacturers, and businesses, as well as service providers such as doctors and dentists. These individuals

QUICK Q&A

Is inflation always a bad thing?

No. Inflation can be very good for the economy. It can mean that businesses are making good profits. This means there is a good amount of money being spent and used on the open market.

When there's inflation, does that mean the prices of all goods are rising?

Not necessarily. Inflation might mean that some products and services have increased in price, while prices for other products and services remain the same or even decrease. Also, some prices for products and services might be rising, but the products and services might have new value-added features (like DVD players in new cars) that account for at least some of the price increase. A period of inflation features price increases for a large number of—but not necessarily all—popular goods and services over an extended period of time.

Do higher inflation rates mean higher wages and salaries for workers?

Just because the economy is experiencing inflation does not mean that workers will receive higher wages to keep up with that inflation. Sometimes, company owners can't afford to increase the wages of their workers, even if inflation has helped the company owners to earn bigger profits. During an inflationary period, company owners often have to pay higher prices for the materials and services that they have to buy in order to keep their companies in business. This leaves them with less money with which to offer raises to their employees.

collect as much information about goods and services as they can. They gather information about the prices being charged, as well as how many products the company or organization sells. These workers, called economic assistants, record the prices of about eighty thousand different items each month. They not only collect the prices of items but also take note of the quantities in which items are sold—such as the size of a can of soda or a box of cereal. They do this so the prices recorded are as accurate as possible.

For example, an economic assistant named Anna notices that a can of soda costs $1.50, the same price that it cost a year ago. However, Anna thinks the can of soda looks different, so she checks the amount of soda in the can and discovers that the company has changed the can's size. The can last year held eight ounces. But this year, the can holds only six ounces. So, even though the price is still $1.50, the consumer is buying less soda. If you pay the same amount of money for a smaller can, you are actually paying more because the same amount of money buys you less soda.

Another detail that economic assistants look for is a change in value. Let's say that last year a dozen eggs cost $1.45. This year, however, a dozen eggs cost $2.50. This time Anna reads the label on the egg carton. She finds that the same company that sold a dozen eggs last year

When evaluating the cost of something, it's important to take note of the quantity and quality of the item you're purchasing.

for $1.45 has switched from selling regular eggs to selling certified organic eggs. In order to sell certified organic eggs, the egg farmer has to put more money into his chickens. He does this through feeding them better food and providing them with more space, for instance. The customer who buys the certified organic eggs is getting a better product than if he or she bought regular eggs. When a consumer gets better quality, he or she expects to pay more money. So, the rise in the price of eggs was not caused by inflation.

All of the information that economic assistants collect is sent to Department of Labor specialists. These specialists make sure that the economic assistants have not made any mistakes. Once all the information has been verified as correct, the consumer price index is created. The prices of the items in the market basket are compared to similar market basket data from previous years. The specialists compare the baskets from one year to the next to see if overall prices are going up, remaining the same, or going down.

It is from this comparison that the specialists decide if the economy is leaning toward inflation, is stagnant, or is experiencing deflation. A stagnant economy is one that isn't growing or shrinking. An economy experiencing deflation means that prices are going down. Although that may sound great, deflation is not necessarily a good thing. As prices go down, businesses lose money and potentially have to fire employees. The consumer price index is an important measure because it helps the government understand whether or not the economy is in a good place.

Other Measurements

The consumer price index is just one way to measure inflation. The CPI measures inflation from the point of view of consumers. There is another index called the producer price index (PPI). The PPI measures inflation from the point of view of the people who make the products.

Inflation is also measured by the employment cost index (ECI), which measures inflation from the point of view of the labor market (the workers). The Department of Labor also uses its International Price Program to measure inflation by studying the products that the United States imports (buys from other countries) and exports (sells to other countries). There is also a measure called the gross domestic product deflator, which tracks inflation both by what consumers buy and by what the government spends.

Although the consumer price index is the most widely used measurement tool, the government uses all of these indicators to help gauge inflation in the United States. It is important to look not only at what the country's consumers are doing because they aren't the only component of the economy. For instance, in the twenty-first century, the United States' economy is linked to many other countries' economies through trade and manufacturing factories that US companies own overseas. For this reason, it is important to track the inflation of imported and exported products. Together, all of these measurement tools help the United States understand the current effects of inflation.

CHAPTER 4

ITS EFFECTS

An inflation rate of 2 to 3 percent demonstrates that the economy is growing. Businesses are making profits because most people can afford to buy goods and services. These profits are then put back into the businesses so they can create new products, which grab the attention of even more consumers. Businesses might even offer their employees better wages. This makes the employees happy and encourages them to go out and purchase new goods and services, too. It's a good cycle. However, a rate higher than 3 percent can have dangerous consequences.

Opposite: Unchecked inflation can cause economies to unravel.

A Good Rate of Inflation

Let's visit Amani and her lemonade stand again. One day, Amani decides to raise the cost of her lemonade from $1 a glass to $1.03 (a 3 percent increase). Not many people would complain about this inflated price. Another three cents is fairly easy to adjust to. Over the course of the summer, this extra three cents per glass gives Amani an additional $6 profit.

The next summer, Amani buys three pints of strawberries with her $6 profit from the previous year. Then, she advertises that she has a new product. Her customers can buy her regular lemonade for $1.03, as usual. But her new product, strawberry lemonade, costs $1.25 per glass. Not everyone wants to pay extra for the strawberry lemonade. The new product sounds delicious, however, and some people try the strawberry lemonade and love it. Amani loves it, too. Whereas the regular lemonade gives her a $6 profit at the end of the summer, the strawberry lemonade is popular enough that it also provides her with an additional $6 profit, despite being more expensive to make.

Under these conditions, Amani obviously benefited from the inflation of her prices. She was able to improve the variety of her drinks. Additionally, she was able to use some of her extra profits to hire her cousin to help out at the stand, so her cousin benefited from inflation as welll. Amani's customers also benefited. They were able to enjoy Amani's original lemonade with only a three cent increase. The extra money that they paid inspired Amani to invest in strawberries and create a new drink. This new drink was enjoyed by a large number of her old customers and attracted some new customers.

High Inflation Rates

A 3 percent inflation rate is considered a sign of economic health. But if inflation goes higher than 3 percent, a wide range of people may begin to suffer. A 10 percent inflation rate, for instance, would raise the price of Amani's original lemonade from $1 to $1.10 per glass. Some people could afford this inflated price because the money they make might have also increased. But the 10 percent hike in price might be too high for other people. Some people, like those who are retired, live on a fixed income. That means they receive the same amount of money each year, without any raises. Their income does not keep up with the inflation rate, so what they can spend each year decreases as prices increase.

Here's an example of how a 10 percent inflation rate might hurt someone. Alan receives an allowance of $10 a week. He has received this same amount ever since he turned twelve years old. Alan is now fourteen. In the past two years, inflation has increased the prices of most of the things he likes to buy by 10 percent each year. Since his allowance has not increased at all, Alan's $10 is actually worth only $8 now. He can buy only $8 worth of goods with his weekly allowance because the 10 percent inflation has deflated the real worth of his allowance. So, when Alan walks by Amani's lemonade stand, he has to think twice about buying a glass of the juice.

Each week, Alan purchases a graphic novel. When he was twelve, a graphic novel cost $8. This meant that Alan had $2 a week for other expenses like lemonade. However, by the time he was thirteen, a graphic novel cost $8.80. If the price of lemonade also went up by 10 percent, this meant Alan could technically still afford the $8.80 graphic novel and the $1.10 glass of lemonade. He would, however, only have 10 cents left each week. Now that he's fourteen, a graphic novel costs $9.68. Even if Amani's lemonade remains at $1.10 instead of raising to $1.20, Alan can no longer afford it because of the inflation rate. He is only able to buy what was once $8, which was the graphic novel.

If there are a lot of people living on fixed incomes, like Alan, Amani will have fewer customers coming to her stand once prices start to rise. If fewer people buy Amani's lemonade, she might have to lower her prices so that people will be more willing to purchase it. If Amani has to lower her price, she will not make enough profit to keep paying her cousin to help out. Also, Amani will not have enough profit to buy the strawberries and will have to stop offering her popular and profitable strawberry lemonade special.

Low Inflation Rate

Although a high rate of inflation is clearly to be avoided, a low rate of inflation is also dangerous. A low rate of inflation means that there isn't economic growth. It's a sign of a weak economy. This often means that demand is down and people aren't purchasing things, particularly luxury items. This means that there is less money in the market. When this happens, the Federal Reserve can lower interest rates to encourage more spending. However, this doesn't always work.

For instance, for nearly ten years in the twenty-first century, the United States had low inflation. The country was in a period of recovery after a recession, or a period of economic downturn. In 2008, the Great Recession hit the United States and economies worldwide. Unemployment rose, and hundreds of thousands of people lost their homes. As the US economy slowed, demand for goods and services dropped. People just weren't spending money as they struggled to keep roofs over their heads. In an attempt to grow the economy and encourage spending, the Federal Reserve kept interest rates low. However, this

HYPERINFLATION

Sometimes, there are intense and fast periods of inflation. This occurs when inflation rates are greater than 50 percent for more than thirty days in a row. This has a terrible effect on the economy because the inflation skyrockets. The money people have in their pockets one day can amount to nearly nothing weeks later. This type of inflation is rare, but it is a danger that can happen if a country prints lots of money to cover its debts.

Some countries experienced an intense period of hyperinflation in the aftermath of World War II. For instance, Hungary was so affected by financial and physical destruction from the war that the daily rate of inflation was 216 percent in 1946. Prices nearly doubled in cost every fifteen hours so that the money someone had when they woke up in the morning was worth half as much when they went to bed that night.

Venezuela faced an equally grim situation in 2018. A number of issues, such as a 2014 fall in oil prices, corruption, and social unrest, left the country financially devastated. The inflation rate was so high that the price of a cup of coffee doubled each week and families were literally starving. The bolivar, the currency in Venezuela, became essentially worthless. For instance, in August 2018, it cost 2.6 million bolivars to purchase a single roll of toilet paper. That was equal to about $37,902, enough money to buy a new car in the United States, depending on the make and model. In the same month, a chicken in Venezuela cost 14.6 million bolivars.

In 2018, hyperinflation in Venezuela led to food shortages that caused sellers to sell small portions of goods at high prices.

effort had only limited success in boosting the economy. Despite low interest rates, the US inflation rate stayed below 2 percent between 2012 and 2018 according to some measures.

The major concern about low inflation is that consumers will lose faith in the economy. When this

During the Great Recession, people reduced their spending, which put thousands of companies and stores out of business.

happens, people hoard what they have and stop spending money. When people stop spending money, businesses suffer. The greatest concern of low inflation is that the situation will turn to deflation, when prices and wages drop dramatically and hurt both businesses and the economy.

Deflation

When prices begin to fall, people still don't necessarily rush to spend. Often, people are waiting for prices and rates to continue to fall before making large purchases. Some businesses may choose to further cut their prices in an effort to lure these reluctant customers. In response, other businesses must also lower their prices in order to stay competitive. As a result, businesses may end up losing money on their goods and services during periods of deflation.

Imagine if another lemonade stand opened a block away from Amani's and started selling lemonade for $0.80 a glass. Amani might have to lower her prices. The lower rate would allow her to attract more customers. However, if Amani started to sell each glass for $0.75 when a whole pitcher of ten glasses costs her $5.00 to make, then she would only be making a $2.50 profit. That's half of what she used to make when she was selling each

During the Great Depression, so many people were without jobs that organizations like the St. Peter's Mission, pictured here, handed out bread to people who couldn't afford food and other essentials.

glass of lemonade for $1. With that reduced profit, Amani may not be able to afford to pay her cousin anymore.

For businesses, the loss of money or the inability to turn a profit often means they have to fire employees in order to pay their bills. It doesn't matter how low prices are if people lose their jobs, which means that prices will continue to drop in order to tempt more people to purchase. As prices continue to drop, there may be more unemployment, and with more unemployment, fewer people have enough money to buy goods and services from businesses. For these reasons, deflation can become a dangerous and vicious cycle that leaves the economy in a terrible place.

A Delicate Balance

As you can see, it requires a lot of fine-tuning to make sure that inflation remains at a healthy rate. Those in positions of power can do this in a number of ways.

CHAPTER 5

HOW IT'S REGULATED

When inflation is high, one of the usual causes is that there is too much money circulating in the marketplace. During inflationary periods, people have a lot of money and the demand for goods and services is very high, though the supply is low. When one hundred people want to buy one glass of lemonade, in other words, Amani could probably ask $20 for the glass and receive it because so many people want that glass of lemonade. In order to avoid inflation getting to such dangerous levels, there are several things the government can do.

Opposite: The key to a healthy economy is people being able to afford not only what they need but what they want.

Interest Rates

Interest rates are one way to control inflation. These interest rates affect more than bank loans. They also affect credit cards. Using credit cards is similar to taking out a bank loan. Interest rates on a credit card also rise and fall. When the rates are low, people use credit cards to buy new washing machines, televisions, DVD players, and other expensive items. Some people use credit cards to pay for airline tickets and hotels when they go on vacations. However, when interest rates are

Sometimes people use credit cards to purchase goods and services when they do not have the cash on hand. This means, however, that they have to pay back the bank with interest.

high, consumers might find that it is very difficult to pay off their credit card debt.

When consumers see how much they have to pay to get out from under their credit card debt, they would be wise to stop buying goods and services until their debt is paid off. If a lot of people are in debt, and they use their money to pay off their bills instead of buying new products, then the demand for goods and services diminishes. And as you know by now, that means prices should begin to fall and inflationary pressures will decrease. If prices and spending levels fall too low, the Federal Reserve may lower interest rates to kick-start the slowing economy by encouraging borrowing and spending. These lower rates would make it easier to obtain money, as well as easier to pay down debt.

Wage Increases

Inflation is not felt as deeply when workers' wages keep up with the inflation rate. So when workers notice that the paychecks they bring home are no longer enough to pay for their house, food, and clothing, they might go to their bosses and ask for more money.

When salaries keep up with inflation, then increases in wages help to control inflation. Although inflation continues to rise, so, too, do workers' salaries, so no financial pain is felt.

Annual pay raises are important to help people keep up with the annual rate of inflation.

The Bottom Line

If inflation is controlled, it can stimulate the economy and provide profits for businesses and raises in wages for workers. However, if inflation is not controlled, it can send prices so high that buying a loaf of bread can become as dramatic an event as buying a car. This can especially be the case when a country experiences hyperinflation, when prices spike and continue to rise for an extended period of time.

Keeping inflation at a reasonable rate is partially the responsibility of the Federal Reserve, which sets the interest rates for banks. However, individuals play a significant role in inflation. Individuals affect supply and demand as they decide what to buy and when to avoid spending money. When inflation gets too high, people stop buying goods and services that they do not really need. As the demand for goods and services drops, prices usually also drop. This can inspire consumers to spend money again.

In the end, inflation is neither all good nor all bad. It has its benefits and its dangers. One thing that is for certain, however, is that it is here to stay. Navigating the upward swells of inflation and the sudden plummets of deflation, the big waves of a soaring and crashing economy, can be a scary thrill ride. It requires a calm mind, a cool head, and careful planning.

So, how can you plan for inflation without knowing what inflation will look like in the future? Saving money is always a good plan. Putting part of your allowance, paycheck, or birthday gifts in a savings account is a good first step. An important second step is to only use this money in case of emergencies. You will have a sense of security and the reassuring knowledge that you can

A FEW MORE FACTS

- People who work often receive an increase each year from their bosses. These yearly raises in salary or wages often help to account for the rate of inflation. This means that the prices don't seem higher because people's salaries are keeping up with the rate of inflation. Over time, however, this means the average price of goods and services also increases at a steady rate. For instance, in May 1980, grade-A eggs cost approximately $0.74 per dozen. In May 2018, the same eggs cost $1.98 per dozen. This is nearly a 170 percent increase in the price of eggs in a period of about forty years.

- In the twenty-first century, most countries' economies are greatly impacted by international trade. For these reasons, there is a global inflation rate in addition to national ones.

- Like Venezuela, Zimbabwe experienced a couple periods of hyperinflation in the twenty-first century. For instance, its annual rate of inflation was nearly 400 percent in 2017.

ride out whatever economic rough waters have been stirred up. You do not have to be a helpless victim of the economy's ups and downs. Instead, you can manage and spend your money wisely. You can protect yourself from the uncertainty and panic that often grips the markets and focus instead on calmly enjoying your security and planning for the future and the kind of life you would like to create for yourself.

GLOSSARY

barter To trade goods or services for other goods and services without the exchange of money.

consumer price index (CPI) A measurement of the prices of goods and services people buy.

cost-push inflation The increase in prices of goods and services that results from higher production costs.

currency Money in any form that is used as a medium of exchange, especially circulating paper money.

deflation A steady decrease in the level of consumer prices.

demand-pull inflation The increase in prices that results from more people wanting to buy goods and services.

devalue To lessen the value of something. When a country prints too much money, its currency becomes devalued.

Federal Reserve The central controlling bank of the United States that sets the rules by which all other US banks function.

fixed income The amount of money an individual makes that remains constant, regardless of changing economic factors such as inflation.

gold standard A principle in which a currency's strength is defined by the amount of gold in a country's reserves.

goods and services Goods, like television sets or cars, are objects that are purchased and used by the consumer; services, like haircuts or house cleaning, are things that are done for you when you pay for them.

hyperinflation Extremely high inflation, or inflation that is out of control.

inflation A general increase in the prices of goods and services over a period of time.

interest rate The amount that a bank charges when a person takes out a loan.

market basket A group of almost eighty thousand popular goods and services used to calculate the consumer price index.

profit The money that a business makes after all the bills are paid.

profit-driven increase The rise in the price of goods or services not caused by a rise in operating expenses or demand but by a business's desire to make more money.

purchasing power The amount of goods and services that a fixed amount of money can buy.

reserve A supply of something, like precious metals, to be saved for future use.

FURTHER INFORMATION

Books

Kallen, Stuart. *The Great Recession.* Understanding World History. San Diego: ReferencePoint Press, 2014.

Loria, Laura. *Inflation, Deflation, and Unemployment.* Understanding Economics. New York: Rosen Publishing Group, 2019.

Meyer, Terry Teague. *How Inflation Affects You.* Your Economic Future. New York: Rosen Publishing Group, 2013.

Websites

Chair the Fed: A Monetary Policy Game

https://sffed-education.org/chairthefed/WebGamePlay.html

This game gives you the opportunity to act as the Federal Reserve and adjust the interest rate to see how it affects both the rate of inflation and the unemployment rate amid situations like oil crises.

Inflation

https://www.econlib.org/library/Topics/HighSchool/Inflation.html#definition

This Library of Economics and Liberty resource provides an overview and additional resources for understanding inflation.

Lifetime Inflation Activity

https://www.stlouisfed.org/~/media/education/
lessons/pdf/lifetime-inflation-activity.pdf?la=en

This website leads you through an activity that will help
you understand the impact of inflation by allowing you
to see the changes in prices over your lifetime.

Videos

Deflation

https://www.youtube.com/
watch?reload=9&v=ouNKQ1OUnwc

This brief video explains the negative effects of deflation.

Hyperinflation

https://www.khanacademy.org/economics-finance
-domain/macroeconomics/monetary-system-topic/
macro-definition-measurement-and-functions-of
-money/v/hyperinflation

This video explains hyperinflation, presenting examples
from Germany, Hungary, and Zimbabwe.

Introduction to the Producer Price Index

https://www.youtube.com/watch?v=d9Y48rsgZZg

This video briefly explains the producer price index, one
of the ways to measure inflation.

Organizations

Board of Governors of the Federal Reserve System
20th Street and Constitution Avenue NW
Washington, DC 20551
(888) 851-1920
Website: https://www.federalreserve.gov

The Federal Reserve System is the central bank of the United States. Its duties include the regulation of banks and inflation through the adjustment of interest rates.

Bureau of Labor Statistics (BLS)
Division of Information Services
2 Massachusetts Avenue NE, Room 2860
Washington, DC 20212
(202) 691-5200
Website: http://www.bls.gov

The Bureau of Labor Statistics collects, analyzes, and distributes statistical information related to labor and economics. Importantly, this federal organization is responsible for developing measurements of inflation like the consumer price index and the producer price index.

Council for Economic Education
122 East 42nd Street, Suite 2600
New York, NY 10168
(212) 730-7007
Website: https://www.councilforeconed.org

This organization's goal is to educate K–12 students about economics through providing instructors with resources in addition to running student programming and challenges.

Department of Finance Canada
90 Elgin Street
Ottawa, ON K1A 0G5
Canada
(613) 369-3710
Website: https://www.fin.gc.ca/fin-eng.asp

The Department of Finance Canada is the federal department primarily responsible for developing and implementing strong economic policies and programs.

Statistics Canada
150 Tunney's Pasture Driveway
Ottawa, ON K1A 0T6
Canada
(800) 263-1136
Website: http://www.statcan.ca/start.html

This government agency produces a variety of statistics about the country's population, resources, and economy. For instance, this agency provides information about Canada's consumer price index and unemployment rate.

United States Department of the Treasury
1500 Pennsylvania Avenue NW
Washington, DC 20220
(202) 622-2000
Website: https://home.treasury.gov

This government department is responsible for promoting economic prosperity and ensuring the country's financial health. It operates and maintains systems that are critical to the nation's finances, such as the production of currency.

United States Mint
Office of Public Affairs
801 9th Street NW
Washington, DC 20220-0001
(800) 872-6468
Website: http://www.usmint.gov

The primary mission of the US Mint is to produce and circulate US coinage while also protecting the government's gold and silver reserves. It is a part of the Department of the Treasury.

SELECTED BIBLIOGRAPHY

Appelbaum, Binyamin. "US Inflation Remains Low, and That's a Problem." *New York Times,* July 24, 2017. https://www.nytimes.com/2017/07/24/us/politics/ us-inflation-remains-low-and-thats-a-problem.html.

Ball, R. J. *Inflation and the Theory of Money.* Piscataway, NJ: Aldine Transaction, 2007.

Davies, Glyn, and Roy Davies. *A History of Money from Ancient Times to the Present Day.* Cardiff, Wales: University of Wales Press, 2002.

Ferguson, Niall. *The Ascent of Money: A Financial History of the World.* New York: Penguin Press, 2008.

Irwin, Neil. "The Era of Very Low Inflation and Interest Rates May Be Near an End." *New York Times*, April 26, 2018. https://www.nytimes.com/2018/04/26/upshot/ the-era-of-very-low-inflation-and-interest-rates-may-be-near-an-end.html.

Mishkin, Frederic S. *Monetary Policy Strategy.* Cambridge, MA: MIT Press, 2007.

Partington, Richard. "14m Bolivars for a Chicken: Venezuela Hyperinflation Explained." *Guardian*, August 20, 2018. https://www.theguardian.com/world/2018/ aug/20/venezuela-bolivars-hyperinflation-banknotes.

Salvatore, Dominic and Eugene Diulio. *Principles of Economics.* New York: McGraw Hill, 2008.

Samuelson, Robert J. *The Great Inflation and Its Aftermath: The Past and Future of American Affluence*. New York: Random House, 2008.

Swaneberg, August. *Macroeconomics Demystified*. New York: McGraw-Hill, 2005.

Uchoa, Pablo. "How Do You Solve Catastrophic Hyperinflation?" BBC News, September 22, 2018. https://www.bbc.com/news/business-45523636.

INDEX

ABOUT THE AUTHOR

Chet'la Sebree is a writer, editor, and researcher. She has written and edited several books for Cavendish Square Publishing, including one on the Great Depression. She has degrees in English and creative writing from the University of Richmond and American University, respectively. She is from the Mid-Atlantic region.